POETRY
FOR TEACHERS

(by a teacher)

BRIAN TAYLOR

WESTBOW
PRESS®
A DIVISION OF THOMAS NELSON
& ZONDERVAN

WestBow Press books may be ordered through
booksellers or by contacting:

WestBow Press
A Division of Thomas Nelson & Zondervan
1663 Liberty Drive
Bloomington, IN 47403
www.westbowpress.com
844-714-3454

ISBN: 978-1-6642-3326-3 (sc)
ISBN: 978-1-6642-3328-7 (hc)
ISBN: 978-1-6642-3327-0 (e)

Library of Congress Control Number: 2021908753

Print information available on the last page.

WestBow Press rev. date: 5/4/2021

CONTENTS

ACKNOWLEDGMENT

Poems were inspired by daily interactions with students and staff members at the elementary schools in Oceanside where I've taught.

INTRODUCTORY PAGE

The poems you are about to read don't have titles. There were many aspects about teaching I wanted to cover, so the poems have been arranged by topics. I believe these poems will bring your own happy memories of being in the classroom.

The students in your classroom
Are going to learn many things from you
Create a positive learning environment
You'll be blessed if you do

MEETING STUDENTS

The children are down the halls
Ready to enter their new classroom
Meet their anticipation with a smile
With no detection of gloom and doom

Your students are ready for vacation
Their attention in class is waning
Have an alternative plan if necessary
Especially if it's raining!

INSTRUCTION

Books and pencils are on the students' desks
The children are trying to pay attention
They are ready to listen and respond
To whatever you specifically mention

I had a difficult day today
None of my lessons were clicking
Reflecting on my instructional delivery
Will help me to see what wasn't sticking

MEETING STUDENTS

The principal has brought to my attention
A child who has many hurdles to overcome
That child will become a student in my class
We don't know where he came from
I will reach out to this child
I will build a relationship
This child will have a teacher that cares about her
A teacher who won't jump ship

Teaching a child to become a better reader
Is a great goal for every teacher
Being patient during the process
Is the main quality every teacher should feature

ANIMALS

Children love animals
Loving animals teaches them how to care for others
Build this skill at an early age
Loving animals helps children to
love their sisters and brothers

Every child needs friends
Friendships can be developed in school
Encourage your students to look out for others
And never allow bullies on the playground to rule

ILLNESS

Illness is spreading in the classroom
Sneezing, sore throats, and runny noses
You the teacher need to realize
Your day isn't going to be a bed of roses

My principal recognized the excellent
work in the classroom
She handed me a positive note
The principal's words were encouraging
I'm thankful for what she wrote

MEETING STUDENTS

A new student is in the office
I wonder what's on her mind
Hopefully she was given a friendly greeting
And everyone around her will be kind

My students created their own businesses
They presented them in thorough detail
It was exciting to observe these
young innovative minds
Who were determined to succeed and not fail

INSTRUCTION

Children with good manners
Bring joy to a teacher's heart
Teachers are supposed to guide students
To be respectful, caring, and smart

Children are wandering aimlessly
in the neighborhood
Without any supervision after school
These children can be impressionable
And fall prey to kids that "appear cool"
If a teacher is aware of this problem
He might be a positive influence in the community
The teacher can help these children
Young lives are worth saving in which we all agree

STUDENT SERVICES

I hear the students in the cafeteria
The commotion is getting on my nerves
The custodian and lunch duties
are extremely patient
While the cafeteria staff smiles and serves
A student throws a milk carton
Across the cafeteria
The commotion is picking up steam
Into full-fledged hysteria
I appreciate the cafeteria workers
Who cook and clean with a smile
They serve the children graciously
They go the extra mile!

It's the first day of school
Vibrant and energetic children are everywhere
There may be some chaos in
finding the right classroom
But plenty of staff will assist because they care
The school environment is positive
Friendliness is felt on the campus
Problems are resolved quickly
With very little fuss

UNIONS

The Collective Bargaining Team came
up with a salary increase
The salary increase isn't what I hoped for
I'll keep doing my job with excellence
Even though I feel I deserve more
No matter what the teacher's union decides
An excellent education is what I need to deliver
Rewards for teachers come in a variety of ways
We should be grateful for our jobs and not quiver

Build trust with your students
Trust will enhance the student
teacher communication
When you have something important to say
Your students will pay attention

LEARNING A SUBJECT

An exciting science experiment was conducted
That involved the three states of matter
Observing solids changing into
liquids and liquids into gasses
Created quite a bit of classroom chatter
Minor changes and explosions with
baking soda, water, and vinegar
Captured the children's attention on the spot
These science experiments are worth the effort
The children will remember what was taught

Reading stories to the students
Creates a special bond in the classroom
Imagination is developed in their minds
Hearing the words spoken aloud help children bloom

SPECIAL EDUCATION/LEARNING DISABILITIES

Children with disabilities
Need loving advocates
High expectations for these students will help them
Special needs classrooms are tremendous assets

Listen to a child's needs
Respond with a caring tone
Be patient after you give advice
The child will thank you when he's grown

BUILDING RELATIONSHIPS

When students lie to you
Heartfelt talks are needed right away
A powerful nugget should be
conveyed in the conversation
When there's no truth you're left with dismay

Artistic ability is expressed beautifully
In the pictures and paintings on my classroom walls
The pictures and paintings generate
passion and excitement
My students' art could be used to
decorate shopping malls

LEARNING A SUBJECT

Geometry is a tough subject
No matter what angle you take
Deducing where the lines will meet
Can be difficult for goodness sake

Seeing things through the eyes of a child
Gives you perspective on how to respond
Lift up the child's spirit
Your words of wisdom will carry
him above and beyond

Commotion is occurring at the water fountain
Kids are squirting water at each other
Break it up before it gets out of hand
Encourage kids to apologize to one another

Parent teacher conferences begin this week
Preparation of children's files are complete
When parents enter the classroom
They hope their children's desks and work are neat

A special event occurred in May of 1998
Where I changed my lesson plans with no regret
Thousands of monarch butterflies
fluttered in the skies
Children got to observe and chase
them which they'll never forget
Monarch butterflies blended in perfectly
with the blazing hot sun
Everything in the atmosphere
appeared so irridescent
Beautiful memories were created that day
Children appreciating nature was
an afternoon well spent

Holidays provide wonderful moments
To discuss the students' family traditions
Show respect for their activities
The class can agree that holidays
are times for celebrations

HOLIDAYS

Another holiday is arriving soon
I'm thankful for the time off
I want to have peace and quiet
I don't want to be ill with a hacking cough

I am facing a moment of truth
My lesson wasn't very effective
The students were left confused and frustrated
I didn't communicate a clear objective

CLASSIFIED STAFF

The office staff is so friendly
What would we do without them
Typing letters, answering phones, and
running interference for teachers
All of them are gems

Jumproping on the playground
Can lead to a healthy heart
Teachers and students jumproping together
Helps get the day off to a good start

Valentine's Day is finally here
The children can't wait to eat their treats
Kids still enjoy receiving cards
But they'd rather receive special tweets

Where is the sense of wonder
That children once had
Too much technology is pushing imagination aside
This is very sad
Do whatever it takes
To keep a sense of wonder alive
Wonder is magical and enchanting
It's where children thrive

What should I do
If I have a very shy child
Bring out the best in him
Appreciate his sensitivity and being mild

Walking home from school
Can be very unsettling
Bullying may take place in secret
Caring adults better step in and do some meddling

SOLVING PROBLEMS

The child can't find his pencil
He sits at his desk doing nothing
You encourage him to get to his work
Your message is, "Do something"
He borrows a pencil
Another student lends him one
All of his work gets done
The teacher considers this to be a homerun

Children enjoy organized sports and games
They follow the rules for awhile
Arguments soon break out
Some children play exhibiting quite a bit of guile
Intervene only when necessary
The problems usually get resolved
Children learn assertiveness,
teamwork, and social skills
Don't be in such a rush to always get involved

LEARNING A SUBJECT

Books are fun to read
Imaginations are tapped into
Mystery, fantasy, legends, science fiction
Children are always learning something new
Fill your classroom with lots of books
Reading books is the key to an excellent education
How many books a child reads
Will be a helpful factor in the child's future vocation

Summer has come to an end
Time to get school clothes and supplies
Children hope for a new teacher they'll like
Parents expect the teacher to be friendly but wise

HOLIDAYS

Christmas is my students' favorite holiday
The celebrating seems to never end
Joyous events capture their hearts
The holiday festivities are spent
with family and friends

TEACHING TIPS

When it's raining
Sing songs together
Cheerfulness will spread across the room
Singing helps when there's stormy weather

CLASSIFIED STAFF

Teachers need to know
The custodians and secretaries are your friends
When you need something done
They'll be the ones to help when there are dead ends

The flu season has arrived
The students are dropping off like flies
Wash your hands carefully
And keep your hands away from your eyes

BUILDING RELATIONSHIPS

A student sang me a song
It wasn't very long
The student's voice was kind of scratchy
But the melody was catchy
The student had made up the words
That included butterflies and bluebirds
The song came from the student's heart
She is incredibly talented and smart

It's still vitally important
To teach children nursery rhymes
Nursery rhymes build language skills
They'll be in a child's memory for all times

TEACHING TIPS

Teaching is a calling
To build academic and character development
Excellent teachers know what each student needs
Teachers make better educational decisions
than the Federal Government

Teachers always know
When it's time for "popcorn" activities
"Popcorn activities are fun quick academic games
They can help spot student academic abilities

SPECIAL EVENTS/ASSEMBLIES

Assemblies shouldn't be eliminated
Schools have them throughout the year
Assemblies serve a tremendous purpose
Memories of what the children have seen hold dear
Assemblies offer something new and exciting
Assemblies have amazing speakers
They add enrichment to a child's education
Subject matter at assemblies can help
students become dreamers and leaders

My teachers gave me advice for research reports
Make sure you stick to the facts
Read carefully when you cite your information
Improper research can leave negative impacts

BUILDING RELATIONSHIPS

High fives and fist pumps
Allow students and teachers to make a connection
Students will do better in the classroom
When the teacher expresses kindness and affection

My time in kindergarten
Was a very special time
I'll always remember the special activities
Such as reciting old nursery rhymes
Riding a tricycle
Being pulled in a red wagon
Painting on an easel
Singing "Puff the Magic Dragon"
I learned how to count to one hundred
The alphabet was a cinch
Writing simple sentences
Understanding measurement to one inch
Kindergarten was a wonderful experience
You're taught kindness and how to share
Common decency and cooperation
skills are critical at this age
Kindergarten isn't daycare

LEARNING A SUBJECT

Music instruments can light a spark
That will help students succeed in school
Learning an instrument plays a
critical role in education
School districts eliminating music
programs are acting like fools

Picture Day has arrived
Kids select which clothes to wear
The photographer makes sure kids are smiling
And that the kids have combed their hair

Picture Day has arrived
The kids are nicely dressed
Several photos are taken
Parents choose which ones are the best

Skip Counting is a fun way to multiply
It makes multiplying not so hard
Learning the multiplication tables
can be done creatively
You can recite them aloud using flashcards

Eye Witness books are captivating
They definitely grab kids attention
The pictures and information are fascinating
They inspire kids to build new inventions

Teachers have always used whistles
Kids hear whistles and stop what they're doing
Teachers use whistles as cueing
signals for important messages
Going over rules with a whistle is worth reviewing

If something is happening in a child's life
Investigate if something is wrong
Find solutions to help the child
Don't let problems drag on

The bell is ringing
Kids hasten to class
Greet the teachers politely
Do what your told without any sass

You'll enjoy your students
Even when they act like nuisances
They'll make mistakes and cause
you a few heartaches
Deal immediately when there's imprudence

New things to learn today
Academic goals to reach
A good education can offer great opportunities
These are the reasons why we teach

If you want children to read
Share books that you enjoyed with children
Read aloud to children daily
Don't keep the love of reading hidden

A bloody nose
A bad stomach ache
A scrape from an injury
Ongoing heartache
Who will provide the Band-Aid?
Who will help when the pain gets worse?
There's someone who's sensitive and caring
It's none other than the school nurse
The school nurse does the work of a doctor
The school nurse is a counselor
The school nurse is always available
The school nurse cares for others who suffer

Don't run on the blacktop
Walk in the halls
Don't cut in line
Stop hogging the ball
These school rules have been around forever
You remember them no matter how old you are
School rules are passed down to generations
Obeying them got you a sticker with a gold star

Play classical music
When you want students to concentrate
Students will be more attentive
What a great way to accelerate what you educate

LEARNING A SUBJECT

Taking notes in the elementary grades
Will be helpful preparation for high school
Taking notes requires focusing on the information
It can be a valuable academic tool

The spoken words to children
Will stay with them in their minds
The words children remember the most
Are the ones that were kind

Children love to share stories about their pets
Sharing pet stories can build a bond
between teacher and student
These shared stories in class
<u>Just might help children make some</u>
<u>academic improvement</u>

Service dogs are great companions
When students are reading
Service dogs teach kids to be empathetic to others
Service dogs are helpful for whatever
students are needing

Stormy weather can be scary for young children
The thunder and lightning are too loud
Comfort children with a peaceful activity
Instead of having them look at the ominous clouds

All teachers wait for that moment
When that student grasps the concept you taught
There's a sparkle in the student's eyes
For that moment, you and the student hit the jackpot

Be crystal clear
When setting expectations
Academic success will be obtained
Making a smoother path to their future destination

Be aware of the quiet child
Who keeps everything locked up inside his heart
The child may be carrying emotional pain
His world might be falling apart
Do what must be done
Help the child right away
Be an advocate and his voice
Have a care team in place without delay

TEACHING TIPS

Consider the colors in your classroom
Do they promote tranquility?
Colors shouldn't overstimulate
Certain colors can aggravate a learning ability

Children should write poems at an early age
Encourage the children to recite poems on stage
Poetry is creative written expression
The child's words may just make an impression

Think, pair, and share will develop
children's communication skills
Children come up with their own
thoughts and opinions
Think, pair, and share allows all students
to be involved in the discussions
Child can state their positions

SPECIAL EVENTS/ASSEMBLIES

Putting on a school play
Is a gift of love to the community
Being involved in theater work as
a performer or stage hand
Provides these students with a
wonderful opportunity

CLASSIFIED STAFF

Aides are a great support to teachers
Every teacher should have an aide
Aides can reinforce academic excellence
Teachers with aides may see positive
changes in students' grades

SPECIAL EVENTS/ASSEMBLIES

The monthly firedrill has arrived
The blaring alarm sound that all kids recognize
Teachers need to keep the kids
quiet walking down the halls
Since the kids are outside they might as well exercise

STUDENT INTERACTION

A former student came to see me
Discussing what she should do when she graduates
I ask her where her passion lies
She enjoys several things she states
The student loves art
She especially enjoys designing t-shirts
People have complimented her designing talents
"I will design clothes," she asserts

Teachers don't want to be replaced by robots
Children crave for teacher interaction
Robots can't express empathy or compassion
Only teachers can express genuine
love to a child's satisfaction

Counting to 100 really fast
Is exciting for most girls and boys
Students love to show off their knowledge
Teachers don't consider this counting as noise

Small reading groups are essential
To ascertain the skills that need to be taught
Whole group instruction only
won't reach all students
Teachers need to eliminate that crazy thought

The child who thinks outside the box
Might be the next greatest inventor
Give opportunities for these ideas to be heard
The child will need an encouraging mentor

Children with disabilities
Have God-given gifts and abilities
The best thing a teacher can do
Turn these disabilities into possibilities

STUDENT INTERACTION

When a teacher is having a difficult day
A student will often write you a positive note
The note is given at just the right moment
You cherish what the student wrote

On the first day of school
Something always happens that
takes you by surprise
One thing you can always expect
Returning students you recognize

PHYSICAL EDUCATION

Physical education should be done everyday
Children will get plenty of exercise
Exposure to different sports is good for kids
Kids have more fun in P.E. then they realize

If homework becomes just busy work
There's no academic value
A bunch of worksheets defeats
the purpose of homework
Teachers know this is absolutely true

BUILDING RELATIONSHIPS

Making a new friend
Will help a child enjoy school
School friendships can last a lifetime
If they remember the Golden Rule

Do you remember playing on the school playground?
Crossing the monkey bars, swinging,
and going down the slide
Playground equipment has basically stayed the same
Students look forward to recess playing outside

Knowing the meaning of words
Isn't just for nerds
Kids used to look up words in a dictionary
Now they use GOOGLE which has
become quite customary

BUILDING RELATIONSHIPS

Be kind to your students
Show appreciation for them everyday
Have fun with your class
Listen to what they say

INSTRUCTION

Teachers provide an education
By delivering direct instruction
Teachers wear many hats
While abiding by the guidelines of bureaucrats

The encyclopedia is still great for research
It's not a book to besmirch
The encyclopedia has colorful graphics
and helpful information
Too bad the encyclopedia is no
longer in wide circulation

LEARNING A SUBJECT

Cursive writing is a worthwhile skill
Children don't consider it a boring drill
Children really like the cursive font
Learning cursive in third grade is
what the children want

Printed in the United States
by Baker & Taylor Publisher Services